Ture Aittola
Fund

Rourke's World of Science

ENCYCLOPEDIA

Volume 4

Earth Science

By Tim Clifford
Editorial Consultant
Luana Mitten
Project Editor
Kurt Sturm

Rourke

Publishing LLC
Vero Beach, Florida 32964

www.rourkepublishing.com

Photo credits: Page 4 © Vera Bogaerts; Page 4b © Jaroslaw Grudzinski; Page 5 © Mares Lucian; Page 5a © Taissiya Shaidarova; Page 5b © George Burba; Page 5c © Brykaylo Yuriy; Page 6 © Arkadiy Yarmolenko; Page 6b © Hiroshi Ichikawa; Page 6c © Elder Vieira Salles; Page 8 © Sebastian Kaulitzki; Page 11 © magali bolla; Page 13 © Khafizov Ivan Harisovich; Page 15 © Charles Taylor; Page 15b © Lorelyn Medina; Page 15c © Alexander Maksimov; Page 16b © David Dohnal; Page 16d © Guojón Eyjólfur Ólafsson; Page 17b © Walter Quirtmair; Page 17d - Nicholas Peter Gavin Davies; Page 18 © Michael Ledray; Page 18b © Chung Ooi Tan; Page 19c © T-Design; Page 19e © Jozef Sedmak; Page 19f © Kondrashov Mlkhail Evgenevich; Page 20 © Joe Gough; Page 20b © oksanaperkins; Page 21a © No Credit; Page 21c © Cheryl Casey; Page 23 © Patrick Hermans; Page 24 © Craig Hansen; Page 24b © Terry Underwood Evans; Page 24c © Aron Brand; Page 24d © Mikael Eriksson; Page 25 © Bychkov Kirill Alexandrovich; Page 27 © Galyna Andrushko; Page 27b © Galyna Andrushko; Page 29 © NASA; Page 29b © USGS; Page 29c © USGS; Page 30 © NASA; Page 31 © Péter Gudella; Page 32 © Peter Wey; Page 33 © Natalia Bratslavsky; Page 33b © pmphoto; Page 34 © Vova Pomortzeff; Page 34b © Jaan-Martin Kuusmann; Page 35 © Miguel Angelo Silva; Page 35b © Photodisc; Page 36 © Allen Furmanski; Page 36b © US Department of the Interior; Page 36c © Dmcdevit; Page 36d © iofoto; Page 37 © Pichugin Dmitry; Page 37b © Richard Griffin; Page 38 © Jarno Gonzalez Zarraonandia; Page 38b © Manfred Steinbach; Page 38c © Viktoriya; Page 39 © Thomas Smolek; Page 39b © Adam Romanowicz; Page 39c © iofoto; Page 40 © salamanderman; Page 40b © William Attard McCarthy; Page 40c © Vova Pomortzeff; Page 41 © Naumov Roman; Page 41b © Nick Stubbs; Page 41c © Susan Ridley; Page 42 © Matej Krajcovic; Page 42b © Jack Dagley Photography; Page 43 © U.S. National Oceanic and Atmospheric Administration; Page 44 © Carolina K. Smith; Page 45 © NASA; Page 45b © Robert A. Mansker; Page 47 © Diana Lundin; Page 48 © Ian Scott; Page 49 © FloridaStock; Page 49b © NASA; Page 50 © NASA; Page 50b © Sebastien Windal; Page 50c © Pres Panayotov; Page 51 © Povl E. Petersen; Page 51b © Valeriy Kalyuzhnyy; Page 51c © Piotr Sikora; Page 51d © Caleb Foster; Page 52 © Dariusz Urbanczyk; Page 52b © Pichugin Dmitry; Page 53 © Cristi Bastian; Page 53b © Dr. Morley Read; Page 53c © Brian McEntire; Page 54 © Brandon Stein; Page 54b © Steffen Foerster Photography; Page 55 © Igor Smichkov; Page 55b © Kaleb Timberlake; Page 56 © David Hyde; Page 56b © Andrea Booher; Page 57 © Sai Yeung Chan; Page 57b © Peter Zaharov.

Editor: Luana Mitten

Cover design by Nicola Stratford. Blue Door Publishing

Library of Congress Cataloging-in-Publication Data

Rourke's world of science encyclopedia / Marcia Freeman ... [et al.].
    v. cm.
  Includes bibliographical references and index.
  Contents: [1] Human life --
  ISBN 978-1-60044-646-7
  1. Science--Encyclopedias, Juvenile. 2. Technology--Encyclopedias, Juvenile. I. Freeman, Marcia S. (Marcia Sheehan), 1937-
  Q121.R78 2008
  503--dc22

                    2007042493

Volume 4 of 10
ISBN 978-1-60044-650-4
Printed in the USA

CG/CG

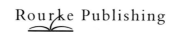

Rourke Publishing

www.rourkepublishing.com – rourke@rourkepublishing.com
Post Office Box 3328, Vero Beach, FL 32964

Table of Contents

What Is Earth Science?

As far as we know, Earth is the only place in the solar system that contains all the ingredients (liquid water, chemical building blocks, and an energy source) needed for life. All the living things we know of live on Earth. It is home to plants, animals, and humans. Everything on the planet needs everything else to survive. Earth scientists help us understand and value our unique home.

Earth science is the study of the Earth. It includes how the Earth works and its origin, structure, and physical features. The term Earth science is a general term that includes all the sciences related to the Earth. It might surprise you that sciences like meteorology and oceanography are both Earth sciences.

EARTH SCIENCES		
Science		**What Is Studied**
Glaciology		Glaciers and ice
Geology		Solid matter including rocks and minerals

EARTH SCIENCES

Science		What Is Studied
Physical Geography		Patterns and processes including weathering and erosion
Limnology		Inland waters including lakes, ponds, rivers, streams, wetlands, and groundwaters
Meteorology		Atmosphere, including the weather
Oceanography		Oceans and seas
Paleontology		Fossils and prehistoric life

EARTH SCIENCES

Science		What Is Studied
Pedology		Soil
Volcanology		Volcanos, lava, and magma

The Earth's shape is almost round like a ball, or sphere. But unlike a ball, the Earth is made of different parts. Scientists call these parts Earth's spheres. The four spheres are the lithosphere, hydrosphere, biosphere, and atmosphere. Hydro means water. Can you guess what part of Earth makes up the hydrosphere? The hydrosphere includes all forms of water under, on, and above Earth.

Earth's Spheres

Atmosphere	= air
Hydrosphere	= water
Biosphere	= life
Lithosphere	= land

This photo shows all four Earth spheres.

NORTHERN HEMISPHERE

EQUATOR

SOUTHERN HEMISPHERE

The Earth's Hemispheres

We call the top half of the Earth the Northern Hemisphere and the bottom half the Southern Hemisphere. The equator is an imaginary line around the middle of Earth's surface separating the Northern Hemisphere from the Southern Hemisphere.

At the top of the Northern Hemisphere is the North Pole. The South Pole is at the bottom of the planet in the Southern Hemisphere. The closer you live to the equator, the warmer your weather. And the further away from the equator you live, the colder your weather is.

Another imaginary line runs through the center of the Earth from the North Pole to the South Pole. We call this line Earth's axis. The axis tilts at 23.45 degrees. Earth rotates around the axis. The tilt of Earth's axis is why our seasons change.

The seasons in the Southern Hemisphere are opposite of the seasons in the Northern Hemisphere. If it is winter in the Northern Hemisphere, it is summer in the Southern Hemisphere.

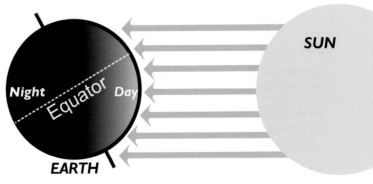

In this illustration, the Sun's rays shine more directly on the Southern Hemisphere, causing those below the equator to experience summer.

What Season Is It?		
Months (approximate range)	**Northern Hemisphere Season**	**Southern Hemisphere Season**
December, January, February	Winter	Summer
March, April, May	Spring	Fall
June, July, August	Summer	Winter
September, October, November	Fall	Spring

Find Out more Did you know Earth really isn't a perfect sphere? Earth bulges slightly at the equator making the Earth a geoid. Earth rotates (spins) faster at the equator than at the poles because the poles are closer to Earth's axis. This is what causes the bulge.

WORDS to KNOW

equator (i-KWAY-tur): an imaginary line around the middle of the Earth

pole (pohl): one of the two points that are farthest away from the equator, the North Pole or the South Pole

sphere (sfihr): a solid shape like a basketball or globe

The Origin of Our Planet

Scientists believe the Earth was created over 4.5 billion years ago. It came from a cloud of dust and gas swirling in space. Some of the dust and gas formed the Sun. The rest became planets in the solar system.

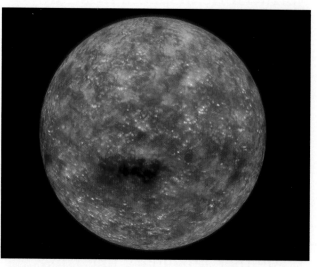

The Sun is the star closest to Earth.

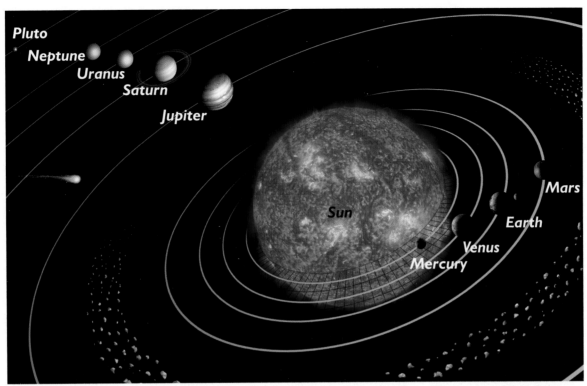

The solar system is composed of eight planets circling the Sun. The asteroid belt can be seen between the orbits of Mars and Jupiter. Pluto, once called the ninth planet, is now considered a dwarf planet.

The young Earth looked very different than it does today. Intense heat inside the growing planet caused molten, or liquid, rock to form. The hot surface slowly cooled over millions of years. Water vapor and other gases made the atmosphere. Clouds covered the planet. Rain helped cool the hot surface. Cooling rocks slowly began to soak up the falling rain. When the ground could not hold any more water, oceans formed.

The land above the level of the ocean formed continents, and the continents have been moving and changing ever since. Sometimes the continents moved together forming a supercontinent before separating again. Pangaea was the last supercontinent. When Pangaea separated, the continents moved into their current formation.

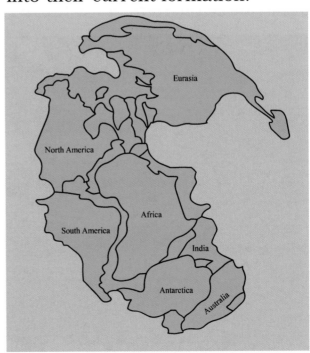

The supercontinent Pangaea existed 250 million years ago.

The continents weren't the only thing changing. The clouds became thinner and sunlight could shine through. Heat and other forces inside the planet continued changing the surface. Ice ages and many living organisms came and went. Over billions of years, the Earth became the way it is today.

GEOLOGIC TIMELINE

Phanerozoic Eon 543 million years ago to present time	Cenozoic Era 65 million years ago to present time	Quaternary 1.8 million years ago to today
		Tertiary 65 to 1.8 million years ago
	Mesozoic Era 248 to 65 million years ago	Cretaceous 144 to 65 million years ago
		Jurassic 206 to 144 million years ago
		Triassic 248 to 206 million years ago
	Paleozoic Era 540 to 548 million years ago	Permian 280 to 248 million years ago
		Devonian 408 to 360 million years ago
		Cambrian 540 to 500 million years ago
Precambrian Time 4.6 billion years ago to 543 million years ago	Proterozoic Eon 2.5 billion years ago to 540 million years ago	
	Archeozic Eon 3.9 billion years ago to 2.5 billion years ago	
	Hadean Eon 4.6 billion years ago to 3.9 billion years ago	

The Earth Today

From outer space, the Earth looks very blue. That is because water covers most of the planet. Nearly three quarters of the Earth's surface is oceans, seas, lakes, rivers, and other bodies of water. The seven continents cover the rest of the planet.

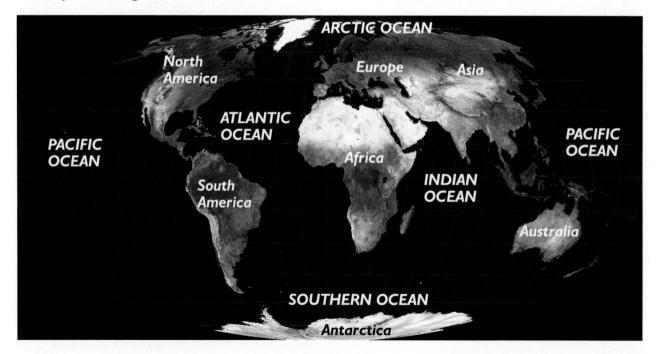

The ocean is the source of most of the water on the planet. It provides much of the water that makes clouds in the sky. Water rises up into the air when it evaporates. This means that it turns into a mist you cannot see. The water comes back down to the ground as rain. Rain fills the lakes, rivers, and streams on the land. Plants and animals need this water to survive.

THE WATER CYCLE

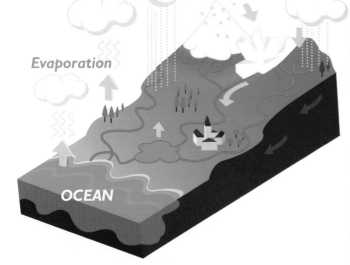

The different environments of Earth support many different plants, animals, and other organisms. Deserts, prairies, forests, and mountains are all types of environments on the land. Oceans, lakes, rivers, and ponds are all types of water environments. Both water and land environments depend on a balance between all the living and nonliving things in the environment. This includes everything from the air and soil to the plants and animals.

Forests and mountains are types of land environments.

The ocean is a type of water environment.

The North and South Poles

Would you like to visit the North Pole? It probably is harder than you think. There is no land at the North Pole, only huge moving sheets of ice in the middle of the Arctic Ocean. An American explorer, Robert E. Peary, is usually credited as being the first person to reach the North Pole on April 6, 1909. Peary, his trusted assistant, Matthew Henson, and four Eskimos traveled over the ice using dogsleds.

Even though the South Pole is on the continent Antarctica, it is still difficult to visit. A polar ice sheet that is about 9,000 feet (2,700 m) thick covers the land. The temperatures in the winter can get down to minus 76 degrees Fahrenheit (-60 degrees Celsius). It warms up to minus 18 degrees Fahrenheit (-28 degrees Celsius) during the summer. Now that's a cold place to visit!

Year round, scientists live and work at the Amundsen-Scott South Pole Station run by the United States. The station, named for polar explorers Roald Amundsen and Robert Scott, is important to research.

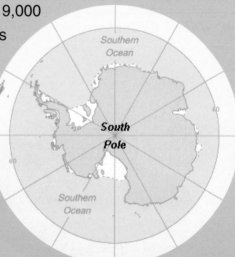

The Amundsen-Scott South Pole Station sits within 330 feet (100 meters) of the Geographic South Pole.

The Parts of the Earth

When studying the Earth, scientists look at the surface of the Earth and the parts that are above and below it. The atmosphere is a part above the surface while the core is a part below the surface. All of Earth's parts work together to make life possible.

The Earth's Layers

Earth is a terrestrial planet, meaning that it is mostly made of rock. There are three major layers from the surface of the planet to its center. They are the crust, the mantle, and the core. The force of gravity pulls Earth's layers together.

Studying how an earthquake wave moves is one important way scientists learn about the different materials in the Earth's layers. Scientists estimate that they can detect nearly 500,000 earthquakes each year in the world. Fortunately, only about 100 quakes cause damage on Earth's surface.

The Earth's layers can move in different ways during an earthquake, causing immense damage.

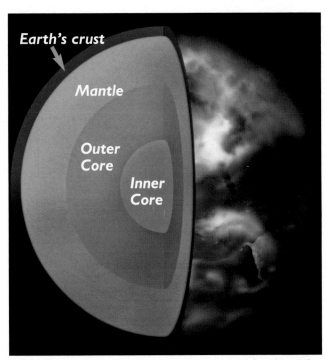

The Earth has a solid inner core and a liquid outer core, which is the source of the Earth's magnetic field.

The Crust

The top layer of the Earth is the crust. Just like the crust on a loaf of bread, the Earth's crust covers the entire planet. This top layer is also the thinnest layer of the Earth.

There are two types of crust. Under the oceans, the oceanic crust is 3-6 miles (5-10 km) thick. Below the tallest mountains, the continental crust can be over 40 miles (70 km) thick.

Forty miles sounds thick but if you compared the Earth to an apple, the crust is like the apple's peel. All life on the planet lives in or above the crust.

The Mantle

Below the crust is the mantle. The mantle is the thickest layer of the Earth. It goes down over 1,800 miles (2,900 km). Most of Earth's rocks are in the mantle. Rocks in the mantle are dense. This means that the rocks are packed closer together than rocks in the crust. They are under the weight of all the rocks on top of them.

The temperature in the mantle is very hot. Some rocks even melt and become molten. This molten rock is called magma. Sometimes magma comes to Earth's surface through volcanos. Lava is magma that has reached the surface of the Earth.

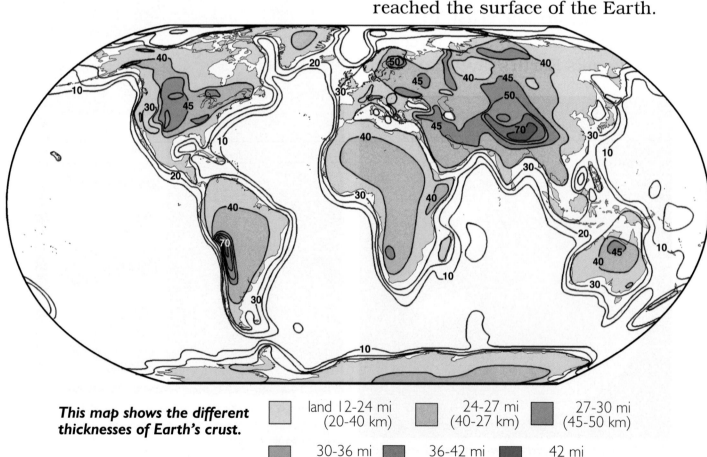

This map shows the different thicknesses of Earth's crust.

land 12-24 mi (20-40 km)	
24-27 mi (40-27 km)	
27-30 mi (45-50 km)	
30-36 mi (50-60 km)	
36-42 mi (60-70 km)	
42 mi (70 km)	

Lava oozes from an erupting volcano.

Find out more

The deepest man-made hole in the Earth's crust is on the Kola Peninsula in Russia. It is 7.6 miles (12.3 km) deep. Drilling began in 1970 and ended in 1992 because the temperature inside the Earth's crust was getting too hot. There were many different boreholes drilled from the main hole. The deepest borehole was drilled in 1989.

The reason for drilling into the Earth's crust was not for an oil well but for research. Scientists learned new information about the layers of rock in Earth's crust from samples taken from the drill.

The Core

The middle of the Earth is the core. The core has two different layers. They are the inner core and the outer core.

The outer core is right below the mantle. It is a combination of the metals iron and nickel. There may even be sulfur in the outer core. The outer core is a liquid because it is so hot.

At the very center of the Earth is the inner core. The inner core is made of solid metal. It is also made of iron and nickel and is very hot. It is solid metal because the pressure is so high. If you were able to travel to Earth's core, the high pressure would squeeze you to be about the size of a pea.

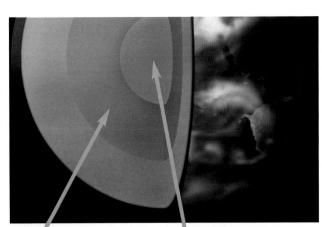

Outer Core
- *Liquid*
- *Mostly nickel and iron*
- *Temperatures from 4,000 to 9,000 degrees Fahrenheit (2,200-5,000 degrees Celsius)*
- *1,800-3,200 miles (2,897-5,150 km) deep*

Inner Core
- *Solid*
- *Mostly nickel and iron*
- *Temperatures reach 9,000 degrees Fahrenheit (5,000 degrees Celsius)*
- *3200-3900 miles (5,150-6,276km) deep*

Rocks

The Earth's crust is made of rocks. The substances that make up most rocks are minerals. The three basic kinds of rocks are igneous, metamorphic, and sedimentary.

Igneous Rocks

The most common type of rock is igneous rock. Another name for igneous rocks is fire rocks, because they form when magma cools. Magma is hot liquid rock that comes from the Earth's crust and the mantle.

Igneous rocks can form below Earth's surface or above it. Erupting volcanos bring magma to the surface. We call this magma lava. As the lava cools, it forms igneous rocks.

Metamorphic Rocks

All metamorphic rocks were once either igneous, sedimentary, or other metamorphic rocks. Heat and pressure caused the rocks to change form. When rocks change from one type of rock into another, they change mineral makeup and texture. The process of rocks "morphing" from one form to another can take thousands of years.

PROJECTS
volume 10
4.1

Igneous Rocks

Granite is usually found in large slabs. It is very hard and tough. Its colors range from pink to dark gray or black.

Pumice is very porous, or full of holes. It is usually white, but can be yellow, gray, brown, or dull red.

Obsidian is a type of naturally-occurring glass. Its edges can be so thin and sharp that it was used in ancient times for weapons.

Basalt is a common rock — it makes up most of the world's oceanic crust. It is usually dark gray in color.

Textures of Metamorphic Rocks

Foliated Metamorphic Rocks (Made of many different minerals)	**Non-Foliated Metamorphic Rocks** (Usually made of one mineral)

slate

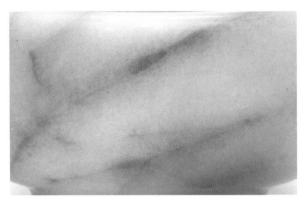

marble

schist

quartzite

gneiss

serpentinite

Sedimentary Rocks

Sedimentary rocks form from sediments, or little bits, of other rocks. Over time, erosion and weathering cause little bits to wear off rocks. Then rain, streams, and rivers carry the little bits of rock until they settle on the bottom of rivers, lakes, seas, or the oceans. The layers of sediment build up on top of one another, pressing the bits of rock together. Slowly these layers turn into rock.

Sedimentary rocks form layers, or strata, in the Earth's crust. Strata near the surface are newer than those further underground. Each layer tells about the Earth's past.

The different strata of sedimentary rock often hold fossils of plants, animals, and other organisms that lived long ago. We usually think of fossils looking like animal bones, shells, or plant leaves. But did you know that even a footprint could become a fossil?

This fossil, found in Colorado, is a footprint left by a duck-billed dinosaur that lived millions of years ago.

THE GEOLOGIC TIME SCALE

Precambrian Era,
from 4 billion to 540 million years ago.

Simple life first appeared, such as bacteria and hard shelled animals.

Paleozoic Era,
from 540 to 250 million years ago.

The earliest fish, reptiles, and land plants appeared.

Sedimentary Rocks

Limestone is produced from the mineral calcite (calcium carbonate) and sediment.

Most sandstone is composed of quartz and/or feldspar.

Shale rock is a type of sedimentary rock formed from clay.

Gypsum is a soft mineral composed of calcium sulfate dihydrate.

Mesozoic Era, from 250 to 65 million years ago.

The dinosaurs appeared, and became extinct at the end of the era.

Cenozoic Era, from 65 million years ago to the present.

Large mammals and humans evolved.

The Ocean

In the solar system, Earth is the only planet that has liquid water. Most of this water is in the ocean. The ocean's salty water covers nearly 70 percent of the Earth's surface. The first living things evolved in the ocean. Today, many more plants and animals live in the oceans than on the land.

Not only is the ocean home to lots of plants and animals, it is important to all life on our planet. Nearly 97 percent of the Earths water is in the ocean. The ocean affects the weather and temperature on Earth. In the summer, the ocean cools the land and air. In the winter, it warms them. How the ocean moves also has a big effect on life on land.

Ninety-seven percent of the Earth's water is in its salty oceans, but most of the water we use is from freshwater sources.

Tides

Tides are the rising and falling of the ocean level near the shore. During high tides, the water level rises. During low tides, the water level falls. The Moon causes most of the tidal movement. The gravity of the Moon pulls the water in the ocean toward it. In most places, there are two high tides and two low tides each day.

dense (DENSS): crowded, or thick

erode (i-RODE): to wear away by water and wind

geologic (jee-o-LOJ-ik): having to do with the study of soil and rock

mineral (MIN-ur-uhl): a natural substance, such as gold, quartz, or copper, that is not a plant or animal

pressure (PRESH-ur): the force produced by pressing on something

surface (SUR-fiss): the outside or outermost layer of something

At low tide, the ocean level lowers exposing more beach.

The Sun also affects the tides. It is larger than the Moon and has more gravity, but because the Sun is farther away, it does not pull on the oceans as strongly as the Moon. When the Sun, Moon, and Earth all line up, the gravitational pulls from the Sun and Moon work together making the tides higher.

Plants and animals near the shore spend their lives adapting to high and low tides. Land at the shores, called coastlines, is built up and torn down by the movement of the ocean tides.

Waves erode rock.

Waves sculpt sandy beaches.

Tide pools are formed as a high tide comes in over a rocky shore.

Waves

The movement of waves also changes the coastlines. Waves break up rocks, coral, and shells into smooth pieces of sand. The waves carry the sand to the land's coastline making beaches.

Many things make waves, including ship's wakes, earthquakes, volcanos, and landslides. But most waves form from winds blowing across the water's surface. Stronger winds make bigger waves. Some strong winds in the middle of the ocean can make waves that hit a beach very far away.

We usually see waves crashing onto a beach, making us think that the water in a wave is moving forward. Waves in deep water are really the forward motion of energy, not the water. The water is only moving up and down.

Tsunamis

A tsunami (tsoo-NAH-mee) is a destructive series of waves. Tsunamis are often called tidal waves, but they are not caused by tides. They can be caused by an underwater earthquake or by a volcano erupting beneath the ocean.

These waves can be small, but sometimes they are very large and cause great destruction. They can travel at a speed of almost 500 miles an hour, and reach heights of over 100 feet. Tsunamis are not like hurricanes that meteorologists track, allowing people to get out of harm's way. Tsunamis can arrive on land within fifteen minutes of a quake.

A tsunami caused by an earthquake in the Indian Ocean on December 26, 2004 killed as many as 200,000 people. It was one of the deadliest disasters in modern times. Because of this disaster, scientists are working to create better ways of detecting and warning people of approaching tsunamis.

The Atmosphere

An atmosphere is the layer of gases that covers the surface of a planet. Earth's atmosphere is about 600 miles (1,000 km) deep. It is very important to all plants and animals. It protects our planet from dangerous radiation from the Sun. It also provides gases that animals need to breathe and that plants need to make food.

Composition Of The Atmosphere

Earth's atmosphere is made mostly of nitrogen and oxygen, with small amounts of argon, carbon dioxide, hydrogen, methane, and other gases. Ash from volcanos, dust, and small drops of water called vapor are also in the atmosphere.

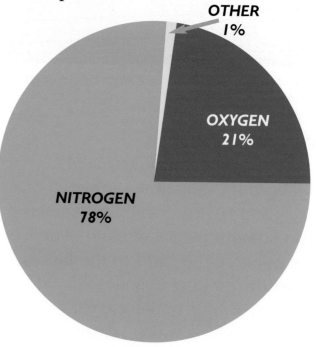

OTHER 1%

OXYGEN 21%

NITROGEN 78%

The Layers of the Atmosphere

Earth's atmosphere has many different layers. The troposphere is the layer closest to Earth's surface. It is where most changes in the weather happen. Half of the Earth's atmosphere is in the troposphere.

Above the troposphere is the stratosphere. The stratosphere contains the ozone layer. Ozone is a form of oxygen that stops most of the Sun's ultraviolet radiation from reaching the lower part of the atmosphere. If you've flown on a commercial jet, you've probably been in the stratosphere. Pilots like to fly in the stratosphere because it is very clear and calm.

The mesosphere is the next layer up. Meteors burn up as they move through this layer.

Then, on top of the mesosphere, is the thermosphere. Space shuttles orbit the Earth in the thermosphere.

The exosphere is the highest layer in the atmosphere, and it just fades into space. Have you ever wondered why you get more radio stations at night than in the day? Well, thank the exosphere. The exosphere reflects radio waves. The Sun affects the exosphere's height. The changing height of the exosphere increases the range of radio stations after dark.

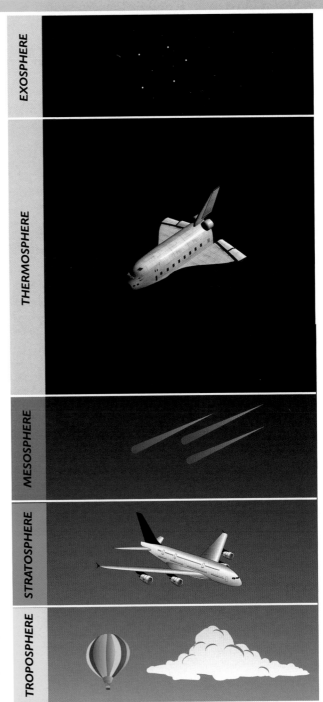

The Earth's atmosphere is made up of five distinct layers (not drawn to scale as shown).

WORDS to know

composition (kom-puh-ZISH-uhn): what something is made of

radiation (ray-dee-AY-shuhn): the sending out of rays of light, heat, or particles

vapor (VAY-pur): fine particles of mist or steam

Forces That Shape the Earth

Many forces can form, or shape, the Earth. Some of these forces come from deep within the ground. Volcanos and earthquakes cause major changes to the landscape.

Other changes occur because of natural forces on the surface. Water and wind shape the planet every day. Human activity also plays a role in shaping the world.

Forces That Shape The Earth

Volcanos erupt when pressure builds; sending out lava, hot gases, and ash.

Sandstorms move huge clouds of sand and dust from place to place.

Earthquakes cause cracks that run deep into the Earth's crust.

Waves erode rock, sand, and sometimes, man-made structures.

Plate Tectonics

It's difficult to imagine entire continents moving, but they do. The Earth's crust is not all one piece. It is broken up into 16 huge pieces and several smaller ones called tectonic plates. These plates make up all the Earth's dry land and the ocean floor.

The tectonic plates move at the rate of about four inches (10 cm) a year. That may not seem like much, but over hundreds of millions of years, the plates have moved long distances. Plate tectonics is the idea that the lithosphere is made of slow moving plates.

Plates come together to form ridges on land and underwater. They form trenches where they separate from one another.

A plate grows bigger on one edge where new igneous rock forms. The other edge of the plate slides under or on top of another plate.

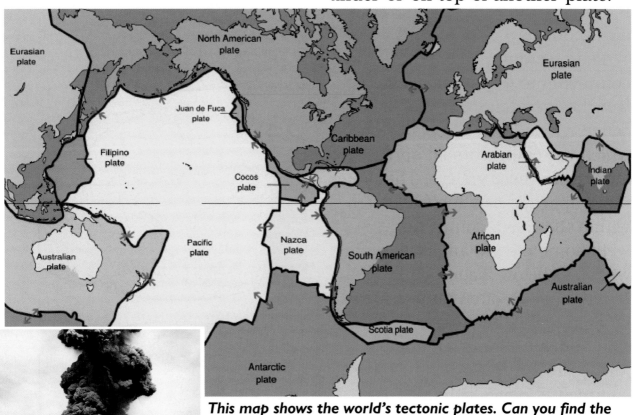

This map shows the world's tectonic plates. Can you find the continents drawn in lighter colors?

Plate tectonics causes earthquakes to shake, volcanos to erupt, mountains to grow, and continents to move.

WORDS to know

continent (KON-tuh-nuhnt): one of the seven large land masses of the Earth

ridge (rij): a narrow, raised strip

trench (trench): a long, narrow ditch

Continental Drift

Throughout Earth's history, the continents have connected and separated. The last time all the continents were connected they made one huge continent, Pangaea. Pangaea means "all lands". Pangaea broke up about 200 million years ago. Its pieces drifted apart over time. They created the continents as we know them today. Continental drift is the process of the continents shifting relative to one another.

Plate tectonics cause the continents to drift. The giant trenches created from this drift are called rift valleys. The plates on which the continents sit spread away from these valleys. The plates move apart as new material from within the Earth comes up.

In some places, an ocean plate will slide below a continental plate. Mountains are often pushed up along the plate that stays on top. The Andes in South America formed this way. Sometimes, two continental plates collide. This causes the plates to crumple and high mountains to form. India collided with Asia and formed the Himalayas.

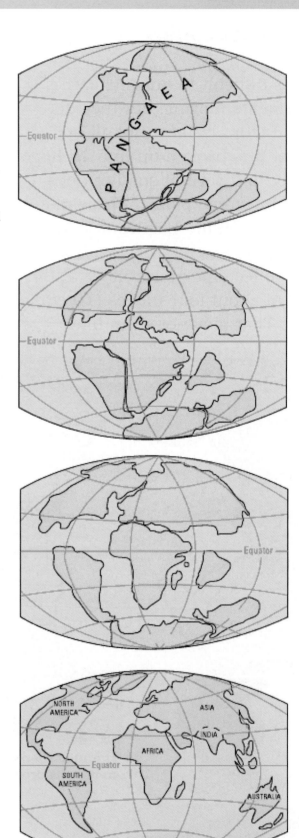

The Himalayas contain the three highest mountains on Earth.

The Hawaiian Islands are actually mountain tops poking above the waterline.

There are actually more mountains under the water than there are above the water. Many of these mountains are taller than the ones we see above the water.

Earth's longest mountain range, the Mid-Atlantic Ridge sits in the middle of the Atlantic Ocean between South America and Africa.

Alfred Wegener

Getting to know... Alfred Wegener was born in Germany in 1880. He dreamed of exploring Greenland and the Arctic. In school, Wegener studied astronomy, meteorology, and geophysics, the study of the forces that shape the Earth. He fought in World War I and was wounded twice.

Wegener is best known for his ideas about continental drift. He looked at a map of the world and noticed the similar shapes of the coasts of Africa and South America. Wegener suggested that they were once joined and then drifted apart. In 1924, he published his theories in the book *The Origin of Continents and Oceans*. Wegener died in 1930. It was not until the 1960's that discoveries confirmed that continental drift really happens.

Volcanos

A volcano is a hole or vent in the Earth where hot rock and gas come out. Magma deep within the Earth puts pressure on weak areas of the crust. The magma melts away rock and creates hot gases. The gas and magma come together many miles underground in the magma chamber. Pressure builds. The volcano erupts when the pressure becomes high enough.

An eruption sends out lava, hot gases, and ash. Lava is magma that reaches the surface. Volcanos erupt in many ways. Some volcanos send out towers of lava and clouds of ash. Other volcanos ooze rivers of lava. Many volcanos explode violently.

Volcanos usually occur on or near the edges of the plates in the crust. They often erupt when the plates move.

Volcanos in the ocean can create islands. The islands of Hawaii formed this way.

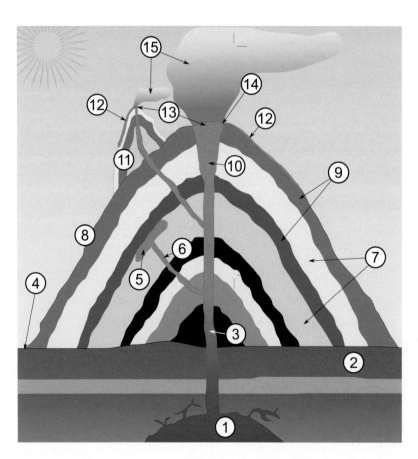

1. Large magma chamber
2. Bedrock
3. Conduit (pipe)
4. Base
5. Sill
6. Branch pipe
7. Layers of ash emitted by the volcano
8. Flank
9. Layers of lava emitted by the volcano
10. Throat
11. Parasitic cone
12. Lava flow
13. Vent
14. Crater
15. Ash cloud

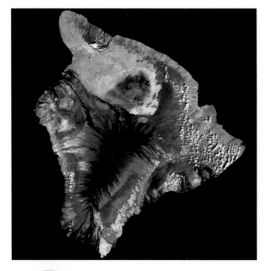

Volcanos on land sometimes make mountains. Active volcanos still erupt sometimes. Dormant volcanos have not erupted in a long time, but might. Extinct volcanos will never erupt again.

The island of Hawaii was created by volcanic eruptions.

Find out more

Mount St. Helens

In May of 1980, the volcano Mount St. Helens erupted in Washington State. It had been dormant for over 120 years. For several months, earthquakes shook the mountain. Steam was seen shooting out of the top. Then on May 18, 1980, the north side of the mountain collapsed. Mount St. Helens erupted! Hot magma and ash began gushing out. The eruption lasted nine hours.

Before it was over, lava and ash covered 230 square miles of land. Fifty-seven human lives were lost. The eruption destroyed thousands and thousands of acres of forest. It also killed thousands of forest animals and millions of fish.

Mount St. Helens before the eruption

Mount St. Helens after the eruption

Earthquakes

An earthquake is an event that causes the ground to shake. A sudden movement of the Earth's crust causes an earthquake. This releases energy within the ground.

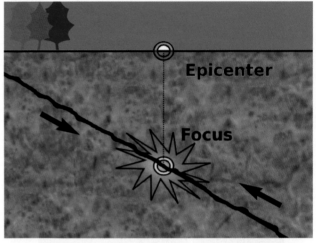

How Earthquakes Happen

When tectonic plates collide, they can cause the Earth's crust to crack. These cracks, called faults, usually run along the edges of the plates. A few are in the middle of the plates. Most faults run deep into the crust.

The rocks on both sides of the fault fit tightly together. They bend as stress builds up because of continental drift. If the stress gets strong enough, the rocks suddenly snap back into shape. They release shock waves of energy. The shock waves reach the surface of the Earth. The land starts to shake. An earthquake has begun.

The focus of the earthquake is the point where the stress releases. The epicenter is the place on the Earth's surface directly above the focus.

The San Andreas Fault is the best known fault in North America. It runs through California for 800 miles (1,300 km). It was the cause of the Great San Francisco

Earthquake of 1906. The earthquake caused massive fires and terrible destruction. It was one of the worst natural disasters ever to hit the United States.

The San Andreas fault marks a boundary where two tectonic plates meet.

Many people think of fault lines occurring near the edges of continents. In fact, faults can occur anywhere. If you live in the Southern or Midwestern United States, you might live near the New Madrid Fault Line.

Measuring Earthquakes

Seismologists, scientists who study earthquakes, have several ways to measure them. If you've heard a news report on an earthquake, you've probably heard of the Richter Scale.

The Richter Scale describes the strength, or magnitude, of an earthquake. It is named after American scientist Charles Richter. A machine called a seismograph measures the earthquake's strength.

The Richter Scale ranges from 1 to 10. Each number of the scale stands for a tenfold increase in the strength of an earthquake. An earthquake that registers five on the scale is ten times worse than an earthquake with a magnitude of four.

Measurements on the Richter Scale	
Earthquake Magnitude	**Effects**
1-3	• Can be recorded on a seismograph, but rarely causes damage • Usually not felt by humans
3-6	• Can be felt by humans • Damage is usually minor • Some buildings can be affected
6-9+	• Is felt by humans • Can cause great damage • An earthquake with a magnitude over six can cause damage for 100 miles • Anything greater than eight can cause severe damage over an area of hundreds of miles

The Mercalli Scale measures how much the Earth shakes. It is named after Italian scientist Giuseppe Mercalli. Earthquakes with Mercalli intensity of I (one) are not felt. Special instruments detect them. Those with an intensity of XII (twelve) cause total destruction of cities and change the Earth's surface.

This once-sturdy structure was completely destroyed by an earthquake.

Glaciers

Glaciers are big sheets of ice. About 75 percent of the worlds fresh water is stored in glaciers. When layer upon layer of snow compresses into ice, glaciers form. Glacier ice is not like the ice that forms in the winter and melts in summer on a lake. The ice from glaciers does not melt away from season to season. Glaciers cover about 10 percent of Earth's land area.

Glacial ice is always moving. It advances, and then retreats. Glaciers begin to move as the ice builds up and becomes denser. Glaciers slowly move down hills and valleys like a river of ice. They can carry huge rocks with them. They often carve deep valleys as they move. Glaciers make mountain peaks and ridges sharper. They also make valley walls steeper. Three glaciers around a mountain in Switzerland created a peak called the Matterhorn.

Glaciers in the Ice Ages

Glaciers covered more of the Earth at various times in the past. We call these ice ages. The temperature of the planet became much colder during the ice ages.

The steep faces of the Matterhorn, in Switzerland, make it difficult for much ice and snow to build up.

During the last ice age, huge glaciers covered about 32 percent of the total land area. Water levels in the oceans dropped over 300 feet (about 100 meters) as glaciers grew. The landscape was changed when the glaciers melted.

Glaciers Today

Today, many glaciers are small. You may see one in a mountain valley where it stays cold and shady. The largest glaciers are in Antarctica and Greenland. These huge masses of ice are continental glaciers. They are so big that they cool the air and water far away from the glacier.

North America has about 29,000 square miles (75,000

square kilometers) of glaciers. Can you guess what state most of the glaciers are in? If you guessed Alaska, you're right!

This Alaskan glacier appears blue because the ice absorbs all colors of the visible light spectrum except blue.

Erosion

Sunlight, wind, rain, and snow all cause the Earth's surface to change, or break down, over time. We call this erosion.

Weathering

Weather causes the most erosion. Wind, rain, and frost make many rocks fall apart. Chemical weathering is erosion affecting the chemical structure of things.

Water Erosion

Water in all forms causes erosion. Ocean waves can erode sand from beaches, create bays, hollow out caves, and change

shorelines. Rain often washes away loose topsoil. Rain can sometimes make hillsides very wet and cause landslides. Over time, rivers sometimes wear away rocks and form valleys and canyons. The Grand Canyon formed over millions of years. The sides of the canyon wall show many layers of sedimentary rock.

A view of the Grand Canyon shows the layers of sedimentary rock.

compress (kuhm-PRESS): to squeeze something so it fits in a smaller space

landscape (LAND-skape): a large area of land that you can view from one place

valley (val-ee): an area of low ground between two hills or mountains

bay (bay): a portion of the ocean that is partly enclosed by land

canyon (KAN-yuhn): a narrow, deep river valley with steep sides

topsoil (TOP-soil): the top or surface layer of soil

Wind Erosion

Wind can also change landscapes dramatically. Sand and dust grind down the surfaces of rocks and other objects they blow across. Strong winds can change the shape of piles of sand, called dunes, in deserts and on beaches.

With very little plant life to help hold the sand in place, these dunes will shift with the wind.

Find out more

Caves

Sometimes, erosion takes place underground. Caves often form because of streams that flow underground. The stream flows just above the water table. The water table is the level at which the ground is made completely wet, or saturated, by water. When the water table goes down, an empty cave, or cavern, is left. Caves are holes that run horizontally underground. The longest cave system is in the United States in Kentucky. Mammoth Cave is 348 miles (560 km) long.

When water drips through the rocks above the cave, mineral deposits form on the cave's roof. They create stalactites that hang down like icicles from the top of the cave. More deposits form as the water drips down to the cave's floor. Eventually, deposits on the floor will form a stalagmite that comes up from the floor of the cave. A column forms when a stalactite and a stalagmite meet.

An easy way to remember the difference between a stalactite and a stalagmite is, a stalactite "holds tight" to a cave's roof so it doesn't fall!

The inside of a cave shows stalactites and stalagmites.

Human Activities

Natural forces have always shaped the Earth. Only recently in Earth's history have people helped shape it, too.

Humans can change the surface of the Earth in many ways. Mountains are flattened, and valleys are filled in. Sometimes, people dig caves in mountains, called mines, to bring out minerals. Cars, trucks, and trains travel through tunnels in mountains. People may carve mountains into monuments, like Mount Rushmore in South Dakota.

Under the sea, coral reefs form on the wrecks of sunken ships.

They provide a new place for sea creatures to live. We construct harbors and walls (breakwaters) by moving piles of dirt and rocks into the ocean. Breakwaters prevent waves from destroying ships.

Coral reefs grow on sunken ships, creating homes for many fish.

The faces of George Washington, Thomas Jefferson, Theodore Roosevelt, and Abraham Lincoln gaze down from Mount Rushmore in South Dakota.

We dig canals to link two bodies of water. Some canals are small. Other canals, like the Panama Canal, are big enough for huge freighters. The Panama Canal connects the Atlantic Ocean and the Pacific Ocean.

An aerial photo of the Colorado River also gives a view of the surrounding landscape.

The Panama Canal, completed in 1914, is 51 miles long.

We move rivers to provide water to areas that do not have enough. Aqueducts change the flow of the water. The Central Arizona Project (CAP) aqueduct is 336 miles long.

It brings water from the Colorado River to parts of central and southern Arizona.

Sometimes we build dams across rivers. These dams create lakes and provide energy to communities. Hydroelectric energy is electricity made using the power of water.

Arizona residents appreciate the water the CAP aqueduct brings.

Dams change the landscape and affect the plants and animals that live in the area.

Weather

We talk about the weather every day, but what exactly is it? We can define it as the state of the atmosphere. The amount of wind, the temperature, the moisture, and cloudiness are some of the things that make up weather.

A thunderstorm rolls in over the grasslands.

Weather affects many things on Earth. Weather extremes usually have a negative effect on people and the environment. Normal weather has a positive effect. Plants and animals need water to survive, but too much water can be a problem. When the usual weather (climate) changes, some plants and animals cannot adapt to the changes and will die off. Weather can be powerful and even dangerous.

PROJECTS
volume 10
4.2

Wind

Wind is moving air. Changes in pressure in the atmosphere create this movement. Temperatures affect pressure. Warm air expands and rises. There is low pressure in areas with warm air. Cold air is heavier. There is high pressure in areas with cold air. A barometer measures air pressure.

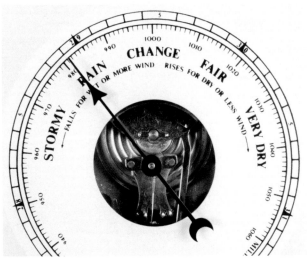

A barometer helps predict changes in the weather.

WORDS TO know

climate (KLYE-mit): the usual weather in a place

extreme (ek-STREEM): one of two ends or opposites, as in wet and dry

moisture (MOIST-chyer): the amount of water in the air

normal (NOR-muhl): usual or regular

Measuring the Wind
You can measure the speed of the wind and its direction with different weather instruments.

A weather vane usually looks like a rooster. The rooster's head points in the direction the wind is coming from.

A wind sock measures both the speed and direction of the wind. It points the way the wind is blowing. As wind speed increases, the wind sock moves upwards.

An anemometer measures wind speed. Its cups catch the wind and cause the device to spin. The faster it spins, the greater the wind speed.

Winds that blow across deserts are usually warm. Winds that blow across mountains are often cold, especially when there is snow. The wind chill factor is how much colder it feels outside when a cold wind is blowing.

Some winds happen only in smaller areas like cities, towns, canyons, and valleys. These winds are low to the ground. Other winds occur across very large areas like continents and oceans. These winds are higher up in the atmosphere. They move clouds. Jet streams are fast winds high in the sky.

A breeze is a light wind. It may move leaves and flags. A sudden stronger wind is a gust. Strong winds can knock over trees and power lines.

Clouds

Clouds form when moisture on the Earth's surface evaporates. It rises into the air where it is too cold to stay as mist. The moisture sticks to particles like dust to make drops of water or crystals of ice. Many drops of water form a cloud.

The moisture in the cloud either evaporates or falls back down as precipitation. Mist, rain, hail, snow, and sleet are all types of precipitation.

Clouds come in many shapes and sizes. Fog is a large cloud that touches the ground. It can be thick and hard to see through. Cloud names come from Latin words that describe how a cloud looks when we're looking up at it.

Cumulus Clouds

Cumulus means heap. These clouds are tall and puffy like cotton. They can start near the ground and extend far up into the sky.

Cumulus clouds usually mean fair weather.

Strong updrafts can change cumulus clouds into thunderclouds. Thunderclouds give off electricity in the form of lightning. A flash of lightning makes the surrounding air expand, which causes a loud sound called thunder. A thundercloud does not always bring rain.

If you visit Florida in the summer months, be prepared for almost daily thunderstorms. Florida has more thunderstorms than any other place in the United States.

Storm clouds warn of stormy weather on its way.

Cirrus Clouds

Cirrus means curl of hair. These clouds are thin and wispy. They are high in the atmosphere. This is the most common type of cloud.

Cirrus clouds are formed of ice crystals.

Stratus Clouds

Stratus means layer. These clouds form a large layer or sheet in the sky. They are usually low in the sky. They rarely bring precipitation.

Stratus clouds look like a soft blanket covering the sky.

Nimbus Clouds

Nimbus means rain. These clouds are dark because they are full of water. Nimbus clouds bring precipitation.

Nimbus clouds mean rain, snow, hail, or sleet is on its way.

Rain

Rain is water that falls from the sky. Rain can be very small drops of water that are almost like mist. It can include some larger drops. We call this sprinkles or drizzle. Showers are short periods of rain that can be heavier. A downpour is a heavy, often sudden rain. A rain storm has heavy rains and, often, strong winds.

A summer rainstorm is refreshing.

A thunderstorm also has lightning and thunder. You can tell the distance to a thunderstorm by counting. We see lightning instantly, but the sound of thunder takes several seconds to reach us.

When you are near a thunderstorm, watch for a flash of lightning and count until you hear thunder. Every five seconds is a mile, and every three seconds is a kilometer.

Lightning illuminates a stormy sky.

A mudslide carries debris to the road below.

Heavy rains can cause damage to houses and nature and can hurt people. This is especially true if it rains constantly over a long time or if it rains a lot very quickly. A flood happens when water rises in rivers or lakes and flows over land that is usually dry. The water in a flood can rise slowly or move very fast, like a river.

A flash flood is a flood that happens quickly in a low lying area. The ground cannot absorb the huge amounts of falling rain fast enough. There is little time for warnings. Flash floods can cover houses, wash away roads and bridges, and drown people.

Sometimes, a hillside gets too much rain and cannot soak up any more water. The top layer of soil falls down causing a mudslide.

Snow

Rain often starts out as ice crystals high in the atmosphere. The crystals melt into raindrops if the air on the way down is above freezing. The crystals stay as snow if the air on the way down is below freezing. Snow is falling water in the form of ice flakes.

Snow falls on a forest of fir trees.

A lot of snow may fall in an area. Snow can block roads and your door. Being snowed in means you cannot get outside because there is so much snow on the ground.

A heavy snowfall can make it difficult to get around.

Snowflakes

Every snowflake is a little different from the rest. They all have six sides, but some also have needles, stars, or other shapes. Snowflakes all have six sides because of the chemical formula for water (H_2O). Larger snowflakes form when the temperature is near freezing. The snowflakes are wet and stick together as they fall through the sky. Smaller snowflakes form when the air is colder.

Under a microscope's lens, it is easier to see the different shapes snowflakes can form.

Sleet and Hail

Sleet is made of frozen raindrops that bounce when they hit the ground. Hail is made of larger frozen raindrops. Hail can fall during thunderstorms. Most pieces of hail are small, but some can be the size of a golf ball or bigger. Large hail can damage crops and even hurt people.

This golf ball-sized hail fell from thunderclouds.

Find out more

Avalanches

Snow builds up in layers on the side of a mountain. Avalanches happen when there is more snow than the slope of the mountain can hold or when one layer of snow slides across the surface of another layer. The snow suddenly slides down causing an avalanche.

An avalanche can bury people. Sometimes this happens to skiers or hikers. Because of this, ski resorts sometimes set off explosives in the mountains to cause small avalanches when no one is around. This prevents snow from building up into a large avalanche when people are on the mountain.

Tornados

A tornado is a fast moving, violent storm. The wind spins very fast and looks like a funnel. Sometimes people call tornados a twister or whirlwind. Water spouts are tornados occurring over water.

A tornado usually forms inside a thundercloud. Areas of cold air pull in warm, moist air. This makes an area of low pressure. A cloud turns around the low pressure. It makes a spinning cone called a funnel. The funnel usually stays in the air, but it can hit the ground, or touch down, suddenly.

The tornado is the thin tube reaching from the cloud to the ground.

Small tornados may break tree branches and street signs. Larger ones can break windows, pull up trees, flip over cars, and knock down walls. The biggest tornados can destroy houses and other buildings. They can kill many people.

Tornados can occur all over the world but most occur in the United States. Tornado Alley, an area from Texas to Nebraska, has had many very destructive tornados. Texas, Florida, and Oklahoma have the most tornados each year. Cold air from the north and warm air from the Gulf of Mexico meet in these places.

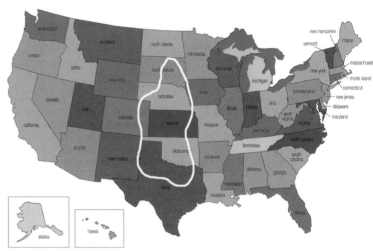

Tornado Alley, circled in white, is an area where tornados frequently occur.

The Fujita scale rates a tornados force. An F0 is a small gale tornado. An F5 or F6 tornado destroys everything in its path.

Meteorologists have developed tools and warning systems, giving people a chance to get to a safe place. A tornado watch means that weather conditions are right for a tornado to form. A tornado warning means there is immediate danger and you should move to a safe place quickly.

Vilhelm Bjerknes

Getting to know...

Vilhelm Bjerknes was born in Norway in 1862. He worked with his father, a physicist who studied the motion of fluids called hydrodynamics.

Bjerknes studied the atmosphere and the oceans. His ideas helped start meteorology, the science of the atmosphere and weather. Vilhelm's son, Jacob Bjerknes, became a meteorologist and worked with his father to set up weather stations to collect information. Their results suggested the polar front theory to explain how a cyclone forms. A front is the area between different masses of air. Bjerknes said that cyclones happen where warm and cold fronts meet.

The Bjerknes crater on the moon was named in his honor.

Hurricanes

Hurricanes and typhoons are both tropical cyclones. Tropical cyclones are powerful storms that form in places near the equator, or the tropics. Whether a tropical cyclone is called a typhoon or hurricane depends on where it is located. A tropical cyclone west of the International Date Line is a typhoon. A tropical cyclone east of the International Date Line is a hurricane.

A tropical cyclone always forms over water. It begins as a tropical depression. Then it becomes a tropical storm spinning around an area of low pressure.

A tropical storm becomes a hurricane when the winds reach high speeds of about 74 miles (119 kilometers) per hour. It usually lasts from five to seven days and slows down when it reaches land. A hurricane often brings rain, lightning, and a storm surge in addition to its strong winds. A storm surge is the water pushed from the ocean inland.

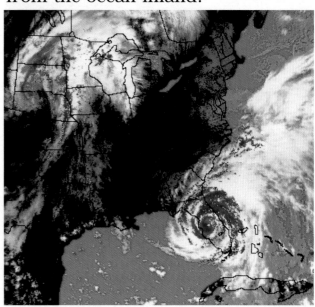

This large hurricane covers most of the state of Florida.

Hurricane Categories		
Category	**Wind speed**	**Storm surge**
1	74-95 mph (121-153 kph)	3-5 feet (1-1.7 m)
2	96-110 mph (154-178 kph)	6-8 feet (1.8-2.6 m)
3	111-130 mph (178-210 kph)	9-12 feet (2.7-3.8 m)
4	131-155 mph (210-249 kph)	13-18 feet (3.9-5.6 m)
5	More than 155 mph (more than 249 kph)	19 feet or more (more than 5.7 m)

The center of the hurricane is the eye. Clouds spin around the eye and carry a lot of moisture. Inside the eye of a hurricane, it is strangely calm. There may be sunshine, warmer air, and almost no wind. Some people in the eye of the hurricane think that the storm is over, but the second part will come in a few minutes or hours.

Strong hurricanes can destroy buildings and boats and can kill many people. The worst hurricanes often form in the Atlantic Ocean. They cause a lot of damage on Caribbean islands and in the southern and eastern United States.

The eye

A hurricane completely destroyed this home.

The Seasons

The earth tilts, or leans, in one direction as it orbits the Sun. It rotates like a spinning top as it moves through space. Half of the Earth tilts toward the Sun. The Northern Hemisphere gets more sunlight when the Earth is on one side of the Sun. There, summer has long days and hot temperatures. Not as much sunlight reaches the Southern Hemisphere.

Half a year later, the Southern Hemisphere receives more sunlight and has warmer weather. At this time, it is winter in the Northern Hemisphere.

The equator receives nearly the same amount of heat from the Sun year round. There are no seasons on the equator. The changes in seasons are greater the farther north or south you get from the equator.

The North and South Poles have only two seasons. The Sun never rises during the middle of winter. The Sun never sets during most of the summer. Much of the United States and southern Canada has four seasons every year.

Photos from space show the position of Earth in relation to the Sun's light at the start of spring, summer, fall, and winter in the Northern Hemisphere.

Find out more

Weather Forecasting

"What will the weather be like today?" People want to know if it will be warm or cold, if it will be windy, or if it might rain or snow. The answers help them decide what to wear or whether to go outside at all. A meteorologist is someone who studies the weather and tries to answer these questions. Weather forecasting is the science of predicting what the weather will be like for that day or for the next few days.

Meteorologists measure the air's temperature, pressure, and amount of moisture, or humidity. They measure the direction and speed of the wind. They also watch pictures of the Earth's weather taken by satellites in space. These pictures can follow storms and show where they are going. Meteorologists use all of this information to make a weather report about what will happen.

Habitats

Life on Earth is delicate. There needs to be a balance between the environment and living things.

A habitat is where certain types of animals and plants usually live. Some habitats are as small as the shade under a rock. Most habitats are larger areas. They may contain many species of plants and animals. Many kinds of plants and animals can only survive in a specific habitat. Look around you. What plants and animals live in your habitat?

The Ocean

The ocean has many different habitats. Some fish swim down in the deepest parts of the ocean where it is very dark. Other fish spend their lives swimming near the top.

Tide Pools

Many plants and animals live near the shore in tide pools. When the tide comes in, saltwater pours into the tide pools. When the tide goes out, most of the water leaves, exposing the tide pool to the air.

A tide pool is a very tough environment. Animals living in tide pools must be able to live on land and in water. They must be strong enough to keep from washing out to sea with the tide. They also must adjust to the waves that crash over them. Many of the animals that live there have hard shells to protect them.

Sea stars cling onto the rocks of a tide pool.

Some animals that live in tide pools are sea anemones, crabs, mussels, sea stars, snails, sea urchins, and whelks.

Coral Reefs

Many different creatures live in coral reefs. Coral is not a plant but an animal. Colonies of coral provide homes for many small fish. They swim in and out of the coral to protect themselves from larger fish looking for a meal.

Many varieties of coral grow in the warm waters of the Great Barrier Reef.

under the sea where there is very little light and enormus pressure. Some deepwater creatures have no eyes.

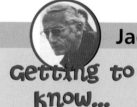

Cave fish do not have eyes. They live in darkness so they do not need them.

PROJECTS
volume 10
4.4

The Great Barrier Reef off the coast of Northeast Australia is the largest reef system in the world. It is made of nearly 3,000 reefs and 900 islands. The reef system is in the Coral Sea and is more than 1,600 miles (2,600 km) long. Many forms of sea life from the tiniest of fish to large sharks live there.

Many people travel to Australia to visit this natural wonder.

The Open Ocean

Many sea creatures live in the open ocean. Some live close to the surface because they need sunlight. Seaweed needs light for photosynthesis. Photosynthesis is how plants convert sunlight into food. Seaweed never grows deep where light cannot reach it. Other creatures have adapted to live deep

Jacques Cousteau

Getting to know... Jacques Cousteau was born in France in 1910. He joined the French navy in 1930. Cousteau tested how long he could hold his breath underwater. He wanted to go on long dives. At that time, big diving suits and hoses were used for breathing underwater. They did not work well. Cousteau helped develop the aqua-lung. It was a device for controlling the flow of gases on a small tank of air.

Cousteau studied the world under the ocean. He used a ship called the Calypso as his laboratory. He explored sunken ships on the ocean floor. He filmed sea animals like sharks, whales, dolphins, and turtles. He went more than one mile, or kilometer, down into the ocean.

Some parts of the oceans change temperature. A condition called El Niño is when a large part of the Pacific Ocean off the west coast of South America becomes warmer than usual. A condition called La Niña is when the same part of the Pacific Ocean becomes colder than usual. These changes can affect the weather around the world. Temperature changes can cause some types of fish to die. When this happens, mammals and fish that eat other fish may also die or migrate somewhere else to look for food.

Lakes and Rivers

Lakes and rivers are areas of freshwater. This means that their water is not salty, like the ocean. Lakes and rivers are not just home to fish living in the water. Many other animals live on the land surrounding the lakes. Water fowl are birds that live near water. Many birds such as bald eagles dive into the water to catch fish.

Bald Eagles are skilled at catching fish.

Lakes

A lake is a body of water that is contained within land. Some lakes are very large and deep. For example, the Great Lakes in North America are almost like small oceans. Other lakes are small and shallow.

Different lakes can have very different temperatures. They can have different mixtures of chemicals. These things depend on the surrounding climate and the source of the water that flows into the lake. Lakes getting water from mountain streams of melted snow can be very cold.

The Great Lakes can be seen from space. Lake Superior, on the far left, is the largest and deepest of the five lakes.

Rivers

Rivers can be large or small. The Mississippi River in the United States, the Nile in Egypt, and the Amazon in South America are very large, wide rivers. They flow very quickly and have strong currents.

All rivers have a source. It may be a spring, a lake, or even melting glacial water. From its source, a river always flows downhill, ending in another body of water such as a lake or an ocean. Estuaries are the point a river habitat meets with coastal waters. Estuaries tend to be areas teeming with life.

Amazon River in South America

Swamps and Marshes

Water is always covering the soil of swamps and marshes. Frequent rains or poor drainage causes this to happen. These habitats are very important for the environment. Many types of animals live in swamp and marsh areas.

Cypress trees have knees that grow up out of the water. The knees help provide oxygen to the tree's roots.

The blanket of plants growing in them prevents the soil from washing away. The water also makes dead material decay faster and keeps the soil healthy. Another name for these habitats is wetlands. Some wetlands are huge and cover a lot of land, such as the Everglades in Florida.

Swamps and marshes are very muddy. Swamps have more woody plants, while marshes have more grasses.

The grasses of this marsh provide habitats to many life forms.

Saltwater fills some marshes. Saltwater marshes are often flooded by the ocean. The plants and animals in them must be able to live in different levels of water and salt. Other marshes have freshwater. Reeds often grow in freshwater marshes.

Another type of marsh is a bog. It starts out as a freshwater marsh. Then moving water washes away the nutrients in the soil. The soil left behind contains a lot of acid. Mosses grow well in bogs.

The soil in bogs has so much plant matter in it that it can be dried and used for fuel.

An oasis is a welcome sight to desert travelers.

Deserts

Many people think that deserts are dry places where it is always hot and it never rains. A few deserts are like that, but most are not. Deserts often get several inches of rain every year. This rain may fall in only one short period. Some deserts have flash floods when too much rain falls at once. Other deserts have an oasis, an area with more water where trees and other green plants can grow.

Temperatures in deserts can be very hot during the day and very cold at night. The Gobi Desert in eastern Asia can drop 58 degrees Fahrenheit (32 degrees Celsius) in a 24 hour period.

Some deserts have hills or ridges of sand called dunes. These sand dunes are shaped by the wind.

Most deserts are much more than sand. Many plants and animals live in these conditions. Animals like lizards and rabbits dig, or burrow, underground to escape the heat. Other animals only move around at night when it is cooler.

This desert is hot in the daytime and cold at night because there is little moisture in the air to moderate the temperatures.

This lizard has adapted to life in a desert.

THE SAHARA DESERT

The largest desert in the world is the Sahara Desert. It covers most of North Africa. It is about 3000 miles (5000 km) across from east to west. That is about the same size as the United States. It has some of the harshest weather in the world. Daytime temperatures can reach over 130 degrees Fahrenheit (54 degrees Celsius). At night, it can sometimes plunge below freezing.

Despite the difficult climate, the Sahara is home to many wonderful plants and animals. Ostriches, raptors, gazelles, jackals, spotted hyenas, and many other animal species call the Sahara home. It also contains many species of high grasses and trees.

Some plants and animals have ways of keeping water in their bodies. Camels can live a long time without food or water by using the fat stored in the humps on their backs. Plants such as cactus hold extra water in their stems.

The camel's long, curly eyelashes protect his eyes from the dust and sand of the desert.

Prairies

Prairies are vast grassland habitats found on every continent except Antarctica. In Africa, grasslands are called savannas. In Asia, they are called steppes. Prairies look like a sea of grass.

The prairies of North America are low habitats. Very few trees grow there. Most of the plant life is low to the ground. This helps plants survive when there is little water available.

Strong winds blow across the prairie in both summer and winter.

Grasses provide food sources for many grazing animals. Huge herds of buffalo once lived on the wild prairies of North America. They ate the grass for food. Because grasses grow from the bottom of their stems, they grow back easily. As the herds moved, they trampled seeds into the ground. Their droppings provided nutrients and fertilizer that encouraged new growth.

Many animals live underground in the prairies. Prairie dogs live in packs and dig burrows underground for shelter and protection. Mice and other rodents also dig tunnels underground. Mice eat the seeds and grass that are all around. Animals like coyotes often eat mice.

Many farm crops grow well in prairies. Giant fields of wheat and corn can stretch out for miles. We use the grains harvested from these fields for food, fuel, and other products.

Forests

A forest is a habitat with lots of trees. Animals and plants live and grow both on the ground and above it. There are different kinds of forests throughout the world. Rain forests have many trees tightly packed together. Monkeys can live in these trees away from predators.

The trees of the rain forest provide much of the Earth's oxygen.

The pine forests in the Pacific Northwest have many trees that need a lot of space to grow. They provide homes for birds of prey like owls. It is easier for birds to hunt animals that live on the ground in forests where the trees are not tightly packed.

Insects and birds live in healthy trees and in dead and decaying trees in the Pacific Northwest.

Forests also provide animals with shelter from bad weather. A single tree in a forest can provide a habitat for many other living things.

Many owls make their home in a forest.

Birds and squirrels may nest in the trees for protection. Insects might also find a home in the trees. Some birds eat insects. The tree itself can provide food through its fruit and seeds. A tree that falls down can provide a home to many animals on the ground.

Humans often destroy forest habitats. We cut down some forests to make room for farming or construction. Pollution damages other forests. But humans can also help forests. We can recycle things made from trees. We can plant new trees. Reforestation is planting new trees in forests to replace the ones we chopped down. What have you done today to save a tree?

Find out more

TROPICAL RAIN FORESTS

The Earth's tropical areas are around the equator. Tropical areas usually have dense forests that get a lot of rain, called rain forests. These rain forests are very important to the planet. They turn a lot of carbon dioxide in the air into oxygen. They are like giant air filters for the planet.

Trees in the rain forest grow tall. The tops of the trees make up the canopy. Most of the animals in the rain forests live there. The canopy contains a lot of sunlight and food. It is cooler and darker underneath the canopy. Fewer animals live there.

Over half of all the species of plants and animals on Earth live in tropical rain forests. Sloths move very slowly and eat fruit and insects that live on the trees. Snakes like the warm climate of the rain forest. Birds of all different shapes and colors fly above the canopy.

The forest canopy gets a lot of sunlight.

Sloths move so slowly that algae sometimes grows on their fur.

Mountains

Mountains are landforms rising above the land around them. Most mountains are very different at the top than at the bottom. The habitats change from top to bottom as well. As you go up a mountain, the temperature gets colder, and the air gets thinner. We identify mountain habitats by zones.

The Tree Line

Along the base of most mountains are forests. The forests will only grow up a mountain to a certain point. The tree line is the height above which trees will not grow. Other plants grow beyond the tree line. They tend to be small plants that can withstand cold temperatures and high winds.

Tree line zones are not the same for all mountains. Sometimes the tree line zone changes from one side of a mountain to the other.

Animals living above the tree line tend to be ready for cold weather. Mammals like deer and mountain goats have big hearts and lungs. These help the animals breathe in the high altitude and cold. Many insects survive well in this habitat. Ants and other insects without wings can stay low to the ground to avoid the wind.

Mountain goats can breathe easily at high altitudes.

Temperatures are ice-cold on top of a mountain. The point up a mountain where snow stays year round is the snow line. The closer to the equator a mountain is, the higher the snow line will be.

Mountains in the arctic or polar areas of the world are often entirely above the snow line. Very few plants and animals live in this cold region.

Strong winds and the amount of sunlight a mountain receives can affect the height of its tree line.

The Environment in Danger

Everything on Earth is connected in some way. Changes on land can affect the air. Changes in the air can affect the water. Damage to one thing always affects something else. It is easy to damage the Earth.

Our planet's population continues to grow. More people means we need to produce more food and build more homes. More people means we need more electricity and fuel. The need for Earth's resources grows.

To meet the needs of a growing population, we often hurt the environment. We have caused the destruction of many habitats. Many species of plants and animals are endangered or extinct.

When we cut down trees, we are destroying important animal habitats.

Fires

Fires are one of the ways people might hurt the environment. Fires can burn homes and other buildings. They can burn habitats, too. Forest fires and brush fires destroy trees and other plants. Sometimes these fires start naturally from lightning strikes, but other times it is arson.

arson (AR-suhn): deliberate lighting of a fire to destroy something

endangered (en-DAYN-jurd): put in a dangerous situation; threatened

extinct (ek-STINGKT): having died out

habitat (HAB-uh-tat): a place or natural condition where a plant or animal lives

population (pop-yuh-LAY-shuhn): the total number of people who live in a place

Forest fires destroy habitats, too.

Deforestation

People use fires as a way to clear land for agricultural use. We call this deforestation. Humans do the most harm when they burn too much land.

Currently, tropical rain forests are the most endangered forests in the world. Many species of rain forest animal and plant species are endangered because of deforestation.

Trees are important to the environment. They provide food for animals and people. Trees also provide important things such as fuel, paper, wood, and food. Some tree foliage removes pollution from the air. Most importantly, trees affect the climate.

Scientists believe deforestation in the areas surrounding Kilimanjaro might be the strongest human influence on its glacial ice loss.

Smog

Smog is another environmental hazard that comes from human activity. Smog is fog mixed with smoke and other chemicals. It makes the air look brown or dirty. Smog has chemicals that hurt the lungs. It is especially dangerous to people who have trouble breathing.

Smog makes the air appear dirty and lessens visibility.

Two kinds of smog can develop. One type of smog forms when people burn fuel that contains the chemical sulfur. Coal-burning electric plants emit sulfur compounds. This smog is common in the eastern United States and Europe.

Another type of smog forms from chemicals released by cars burning gasoline. Sunlight changes these chemicals. Photochemical smog is the result (photo means light). Places with many cars, like cities, have this type of smog.

F. Sherwood Rowland and Mario Molina

Getting to know...

F. Sherwood Rowland was born in Ohio in 1927. In 1964, he became the head of the new chemistry department at the University of California at Irvine. Rowland began to study chlorofluorocarbons, or CFCs. These chemicals were being used in spray cans, refrigerators, and air conditioners. He wondered what happened to CFCs in the atmosphere.

Mario Molina was born in Mexico in 1943. He joined Rowland's Irvine research team in 1973. Together, they discovered that CFCs break apart and form atoms of chlorine. Chlorine destroys the ozone that protects life on Earth from radiation.

Rowland and Molina helped to create the worldwide ban on CFCs. It is believed that because of their work the hole in the ozone layer is now shrinking. They won the Nobel Prize for their research.

Acid Rain

Acid rain is rain in which oxides of sulfur and nitrogen mix with the water in the atmosphere. Most acid rain comes from human sources such as car exhausts and manufacturing smoke. Some acid rain comes from natural sources such as the gases released by animals and decaying plants.

Wind can carry these oxides a long way from their source. The acid molecules can travel for hundreds of miles. They can even be carried into other countries. The acids created this way fall back down to Earth when it rains.

Acid rain is more acid than natural rain. It may damage lakes, forests, and soil. Fish die when the water in lakes is too acidic.

WORDS to know

emit (i-MIT): to release or give off

hazard (HAZ-urd): a danger or a risk

Acid rain damages the leaves and needles of trees.

Acid rain can also hurt buildings. Statues made of stone can be eaten away by acid rain. The areas with the worst damage have been the eastern United States and the southeastern part of Canada.

The damage on this building was caused by acid rain.

Global Warming

The Earth's climate has varied throughout the planet's history. Geologists and paleontologists have found evidence that Earth has had periods of extreme cooling. We know that during one such period, 1,000,000 B.C. to 10,000 B.C., glaciers covered much of North America.

Scientists have also found evidence that the planet has had periods of significant warming.

Oceans once covered Florida, tropical plants grew within the Arctic circle, and dinosaurs roamed Montana (150 million years ago).

Recently, the Earth's temperature has once more been rising. We can see some of the effects, some of which are undesirable, others helpful.

- Glaciers are melting and shrinking. Potential water sources are lost.

Grinnell Glacier 1938   Grinnell Glacier 2005

- Some species of plants and animals have become endangered as their habitat changes or is lost.
- Some species of plants and insects have increased their northern ranges. This makes agriculture possible in areas formerly too cold for crops.

Possible Causes Of Global Warming

Scientists are exploring and debating how much of the overall temperature rise is due to humans and how much from other natural phenomena. Regardless of the answer, everyone agrees we should do what we can reasonably do to lessen our impact during this warming period.

Scientists are studying:
- the Sun's activity
- current global warming on Mars
- Earth's weather patterns
- glacial retreat
- ice shelves in the Antarctic
- ocean and sea life populations
- other biological evidence

They are trying to identify the possible causes to the current global warming. They also want to know how much each contributes to the temperature increase.

We know that human activity such as deforestation and the burning of fossil fuels is contributing to the rise in the Earth's temperature.

Burning Fossil Fuels

People burn fossil fuels to produce electricity and run engines. This produces carbon dioxide.

A small amount of carbon dioxide in the air is normal. (Air is made up of 78 percent nitrogen, 21 percent oxygen, and the rest is carbon dioxide and other gases.) Plants use carbon dioxide to grow and to produce oxygen and animal food. When we burn oil, coal, and wood, we create extra carbon dioxide and other gases. We call these greenhouse gases.

Some manufacturing plants produce greenhouse gases as a byproduct.

Greenhouse gases form a layer around the Earth. This layer allows sunlight to pass through to the surface, but it prevents heat from escaping into outer space. Other gases do this too. These include methane and nitrous oxide. These pollutant gases come from cows and other grazing animals, and from agricultural fertilizers.

Scientists believe that increases in the amount of greenhouse gases are contributing to current global warming.

What People Can Do

Governments, companies, and individuals are taking steps to reduce people's contribution to greenhouse gases.

- Car manufacturers are designing cars that burn fuel more efficiently.
- Engineers are creating biodegradable fuels that do not produce as many pollutants.

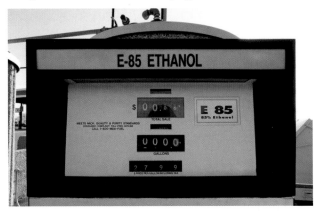

- Factories are continuing to find methods of manufacturing that generate fewer CO_2 emissions.
- Nuclear plants are being built to replace coal and oil burning electric plants.
- Conservation groups are encouraging people to use less electricity.
- Engineers design appliances that use electricity more efficiently.

- Builders use more efficient insulation.

- Farmers are trying to use less fertilizer.

debate: (di-BATE) to consider or discuss something

geologist: (jee-OL-uh-jist) a scientist who studies rocks and the Earth's crust

glacier: (GLAY-shur) a huge sheet of ice found in mountain areas and polar regions

impact: (im-PAKT) the effect that something has on a thing

paleontologist: (pay-lee-uhn-TOL-uh-jist) a scientist who studies fossils

undesirable: (uhn-di-ZYE-ruh-buhl) not wanted, not pleasant

People Who Study the Earth

Throughout history, people have always wanted to understand the planet we live on. They wanted to know why the weather changes from hot to cold and back again. They wanted to know why it rains or snows and what lightning and thunder are. They wanted to know why volcanos erupt and why earthquakes move the ground.

Volcanologists study volcanos.

Scientists decided to study nature. Earth science is the study of the Earth and all the forces that can affect it.

pollution ((puh-LOO-shuhn): harmful materials that damage the air, water, or soil

resistant (re-ZIS-tent): having the ability to withstand

resource (REE-sorss): something valuable to a place or a person

There are different fields within Earth science. Most Earth scientists spend lots of time out studying the Earth. Many of the things they learn affect our daily lives.

- Meteorologists study the atmosphere. They watch and try to predict the weather.
- Some geologists study the history of the Earth by looking at rocks. Other geologists study natural resources such as ground water, petroleum, and metals; all things we use in our daily lives.
- Seismologists measure earthquakes and study the movement of the continental plates. They sometimes try to predict when future earthquakes will occur. Seismologists also help design and build earthquake resistant structures.
- Ecologists try to understand how living things and their environments affect each other. Environmentalists try to protect the environment from pollution and other dangers.

Learning about these things helps people use the resources of the Earth wisely. Human beings must understand that everything they do affects the planet that all living things share.